LERNER & LOEWE

MY FAIR LADY • CAMELOT
BRIGADOON • PAINT YOUR WAGON

Project Manager: Sy Feldman
Art Design: Maria A. Chenique

WARNER BROS. PUBLICATIONS - THE GLOBAL LEADER IN PRINT
USA: 15800 NW 48th Avenue, Miami, FL 33014

WARNER/CHAPPELL MUSIC
CANADA: 15800 N.W. 48th AVENUE
MIAMI, FLORIDA 33014
SCANDINAVIA: P.O. BOX 533, VENDEVAGEN 85 B
S-182 15, DANDERYD, SWEDEN
AUSTRALIA: P.O. BOX 353
3 TALAVERA ROAD, NORTH RYDE N.S.W. 2113
ASIA: UNIT 901 - LIPPO SUN PLAZA
28 CANTON ROAD
TSIM SHA TSUI, KOWLOON, HONG KONG

NUOVA CARISCH
ITALY: VIA CAMPANIA, 12
20098 S. GIULIANO MILANESE (MI)
ZONA INDUSTRIALE SESTO ULTERIANO
SPAIN: MAGALLANES, 25
28015 MADRID
FRANCE: CARISCH MUSICOM,
25, RUE D'HAUTEVILLE, 75010 PARIS

INTERNATIONAL MUSIC PUBLICATIONS LIMITED
ENGLAND: GRIFFIN HOUSE,
161 HAMMERSMITH ROAD, LONDON W6 8BS
GERMANY: MARSTALLSTR. 8, D-80539 MUNCHEN
DENMARK: DANMUSIK, VOGNMAGERGADE 7
DK 1120 KOBENHAVNK

© 2001 WARNER BROS. PUBLICATIONS
All Rights Reserved

Any duplication, adaptation or arrangement of the compositions
contained in this collection requires the written consent of the Publisher.
No part of this book may be photocopied or reproduced in any way without permission.
Unauthorized uses are an infringement of the U.S. Copyright Act and are punishable by law.

CONTENTS

MY FAIR LADY

Get Me to the Church on Time	4
On the Street Where You Live	8
With a Little Bit of Luck	14
Show Me	18
I Could Have Danced All Night	22
Wouldn't It Be Loverly	27
I've Grown Accustomed to Her Face	30

CAMELOT

Camelot	34
How to Handle a Woman	39
The Simple Joys of Maidenhood	42
Loved You Once in Silence	46
The Lusty Month of May	50
Follow Me	53
If Ever I Would Leave You	56

BRIGADOON

Down on MacConnachy Square	61
Almost Like Being in Love	64
Brigadoon	66
Come to Me, Bend to Me	68
From This Day On	70
The Heather on the Hill	72
I'll Go Home With Bonnie Jean	75
Jeannie's Packin' Up	78
The Love of My Life	81
There but for You Go I	86
Waitin' for My Dearie	89

PAINT YOUR WAGON

I'm on My Way	93
Best Things	96
The First Thing You Know	100
Gold Fever	104
The Gospel of No Name City	108
I Talk to the Trees	112
I Still See Elisa	116
A Million Miles Away Behind the Door	119
They Call the Wind Maria	124
Wand'rin' Star	128

GET ME TO THE CHURCH ON TIME

Lyrics by
ALAN JAY LERNER

Music by
FREDERICK LOEWE

Get Me to the Church on Time - 4 - 1

© 1956 Alan Jay Lerner and Frederick Loewe
Copyright Renewed
Publication and Allied Rights Assigned to CHAPPELL & CO.
All Rights Reserved including Public Performance for Profit

ON THE STREET WHERE YOU LIVE

Lyrics by
ALAN JAY LERNER

Music by
FREDERICK LOEWE

On the Street Where You Live - 6 - 1

© 1956 Alan Jay Lerner and Frederick Loewe
Copyright Renewed
Publication and Allied Rights Assigned to CHAPPELL & CO.
All Rights Reserved including Public Performance for Profit

SHOW ME

Lyrics by
ALAN JAY LERNER

Music by
FREDERICK LOEWE

I COULD HAVE DANCED ALL NIGHT

Lyrics by
ALAN JAY LERNER

Music by
FREDERICK LOEWE

I Could Have Danced All Night - 5 - 1

© 1956 Alan Jay Lerner and Frederick Loewe
Copyright Renewed
Publication and Allied Rights Assigned to CHAPPELL & CO.
All Rights Reserved including Public Performance for Profit

24

I Could Have Danced All Night - 5 - 3

I'VE GROWN ACCUSTOMED TO HER FACE

Lyrics by
ALAN JAY LERNER

Music by
FREDERICK LOEWE

I've Grown Accustomed to Her Face - 3 - 1

© 1956 Alan Jay Lerner and Frederick Loewe
Copyright Renewed
Publication and Allied Rights Assigned to CHAPPELL & CO.
All Rights Reserved including Public Performance for Profit

CAMELOT

Lyrics by
ALAN JAY LERNER

Music by
FREDERICK LOEWE

Camelot - 5 - 1

© 1960 Alan Jay Lerner and Frederick Loewe
Copyright Renewed
Publication and Allied Rights Assigned to CHAPPELL & CO.
All Rights Reserved including Public Performance for Profit

HOW TO HANDLE A WOMAN

Lyrics by
ALAN JAY LERNER

Music by
FREDERICK LOEWE

Moderato

Refrain: Moderato

How to han-dle a wom-an, There's a way, said a wise old man. A way known by ev-'ry wom-an since the whole rig-ma-role be-gan. "Do I

I Loved You Once in Silence

Music by
FREDERICK LOEWE

Lyrics by
ALAN JAY LERNER

I Loved You Once in Silence - 4 - 1

© 1960 Alan Jay Lerner and Frederick Loewe
Copyright Renewed
Publication and Allied Rights Assigned to CHAPPELL & CO.
All Rights Reserved including Public Performance for Profit

ALMOST LIKE BEING IN LOVE

Lyrics by
ALAN JAY LERNER

Music by
FREDERICK LOEWE

I'LL GO HOME WITH BONNIE JEAN

Lyrics by
ALAN JAY LERNER

Music by
FREDERICK LOEWE

I'll Go Home With Bonnie Jean - 3 - 1

© 1947 (Renewed 1975) Alan Jay Lerner and Frederick Loewe
World Rights Assigned to CHAPPELL & CO. and EMI U CATALOG INC. (Publishing)
and WARNER BROS. PUBLICATIONS U.S. INC. (Print)
All Rights Reserved including Public Performance for Profit

JEANNIE'S PACKIN' UP

Lyrics by
ALAN JAY LERNER

Music by
FREDERICK LOEWE

© 1947 (Renewed 1975) Alan Jay Lerner and Frederick Loewe
World Rights Assigned to CHAPPELL & CO. and EMI U CATALOG INC. (Publishing)
and WARNER BROS. PUBLICATIONS U.S. INC. (Print)
All Rights Reserved including Public Performance for Profit

THERE BUT FOR YOU GO I

Lyrics by
ALAN JAY LERNER

Music by
FREDERICK LOEWE

Slowly, with feeling

This is hard to say, but as I wandered through the lea I felt for just a fleeting moment that I suddenly was free of being lonely; Then I closed my eyes and saw the very reason why.

There but for You Go I - 3 - 1

© 1947 (Renewed 1975) Alan Jay Lerner and Frederick Loewe
World Rights Assigned to CHAPPELL & CO. and EMI U CATALOG INC. (Publishing)
and WARNER BROS. PUBLICATIONS U.S. INC. (Print)
All Rights Reserved including Public Performance for Profit

WAITIN' FOR MY DEARIE

BEST THINGS

Lyrics by
ALAN JAY LERNER

Music by
ANDRÉ PREVIN

1. The earth is pure muck,___ (Muck's a good thing)___ And
(2.) There's more than just gold___ (Gold is e-nough)___ That's

ooz-in' with mud.___ (Mud is just fine)___ It's drown-in' in bog,___
bu-ried be-low.___ (Beau-ti-ful gold)___ There's seed in the ground___

© 1969 Alan Jay Lerner and Chappell & Co.
Copyright Renewed
All Rights Reserved including Public Performance for Profit

GOLD FEVER

Lyrics by
ALAN JAY LERNER

Music by
ANDRÉ PREVIN

Moderately, smoothly

I would
Once we

give the world to see how I used to be when I had no
all did hon-est work: farm-er, law-yer clerk; mar-ried men and

axe to grind ex-cept for chop-pin' wood. Day was
sin-gle men and some who ain't too sure. Now I

Gold Fever - 4 - 1

© 1969 Alan Jay Lerner and Chappell & Co.
Copyright Renewed
All Rights Reserved including Public Performance for Profit

106

Gold Fever - 4 - 3

THE GOSPEL OF NO NAME CITY

Lyrics by
ALAN JAY LERNER

Music by
ANDRÉ PREVIN

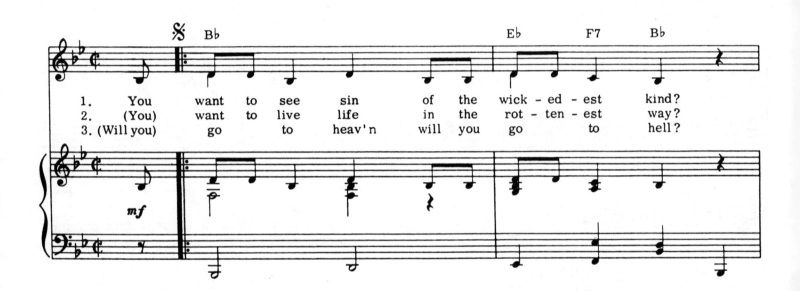

1. You want to see sin of the wick-ed-est kind?
2. (You) want to live life in the rot-ten-est way?
3. (Will you) go to heav'n will you go to hell?

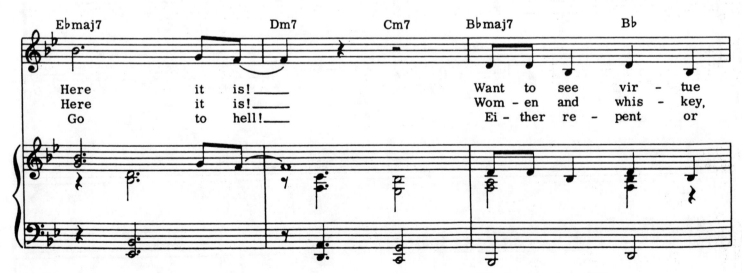

Here it is! ___ Want to see vir - tue
Here it is! ___ Wom - en and whis - key,
Go to hell! ___ Ei - ther re - pent or

The Gospel of No Name City - 4 - 1

© 1969 Alan Jay Lerner and Chappell & Co.
Copyright Renewed
All Rights Reserved including Public Performance for Profit

I TALK TO THE TREES

Lyrics by
ALAN JAY LERNER

Music by
FREDERICK LOEWE

© 1951 Alan Jay Lerner and Frederick Loewe
Copyright Renewed
Publication and Allied Rights Assigned to CHAPPELL & CO.
All Rights Reserved including Public Performance for Profit

114

I Talk to the Trees - 4 - 3

I Talk to the Trees - 4 - 4

I STILL SEE ELISA

Lyrics by
ALAN JAY LERNER

Music by
FREDERICK LOEWE

I Still See Elisa - 3 - 1

© 1951 Alan Jay Lerner and Frederick Loewe
Copyright Renewed
Publication and Allied Rights Assigned to CHAPPELL & CO.
All Rights Reserved including Public Performance for Profit

A MILLION MILES AWAY BEHIND THE DOOR

Lyrics by
ALAN JAY LERNER

Music by
ANDRÉ PREVIN

WAND'RIN' STAR

Lyrics by
ALAN JAY LERNER

Music by
FREDERICK LOEWE

BROADWAY QUARTETS

LERNER & LOWE
Vocal Selections
(0500B)

Shows in this collection are:

My Fair Lady • Camelot • Brigadoon • Paint Your Wagon

RODGERS & HART
Vocal Selections
(0501B)

Shows in this collection are:

Babes in Arms • Pal Joey • The Boys from Syracuse • On Your Toes

JULE STYNE
Vocal Selections
(0499B)

Shows in this collection are:

Gypsy • Funny Girl • Bells Are Ringing • High Button Shoes

FOX
COLORING BOOK
ORIGAMI PUBLISHING

PUBLISHED IN 2018 BY
ORIGAMI PUBLISHING

COPYRIGHT 'ILLUSTRATIONS' 2018 ORIGAMI PUBLISHING
ALL RIGHT RESERVED.'NO PART OF THIS PUBLICATION MAY BE REPRODUCED OR TRANSMITTED IN ANY
FORM OR BY ANY MEANS, ELECTRONIC OR MECHANICAL, INCLUDING PHOTOCOPY RECORDING OR ANY
INFORMATION STORAGE SYSTEM AND RETRIEVAL SYSTEM WITHOUT PERMISSION IN WRITING
BY ORIGAMI PUBLISHING

PRINTED IN THE UNITED STATE OF AMERICA

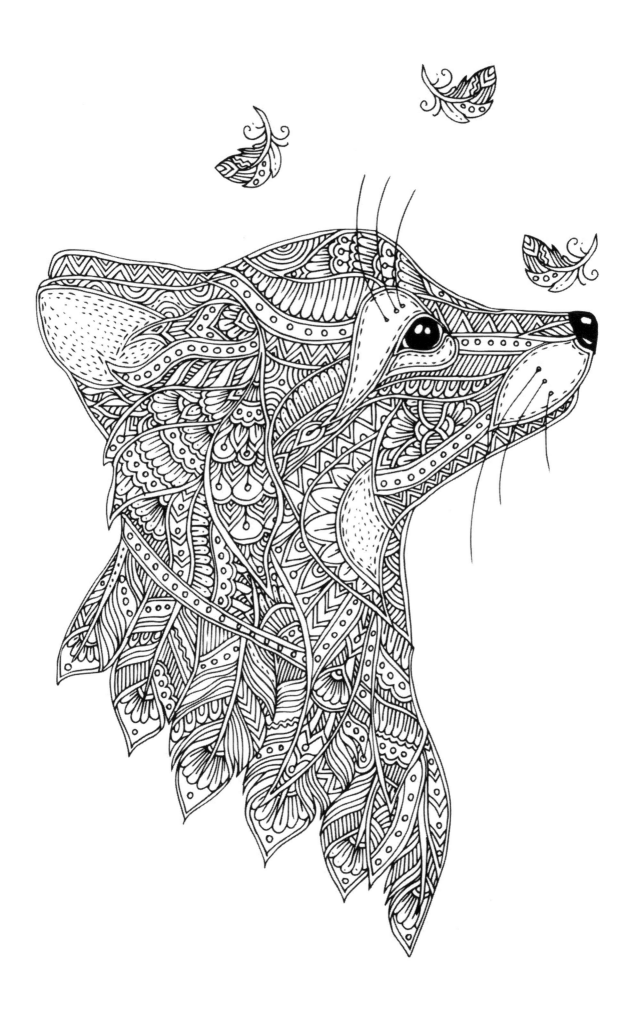

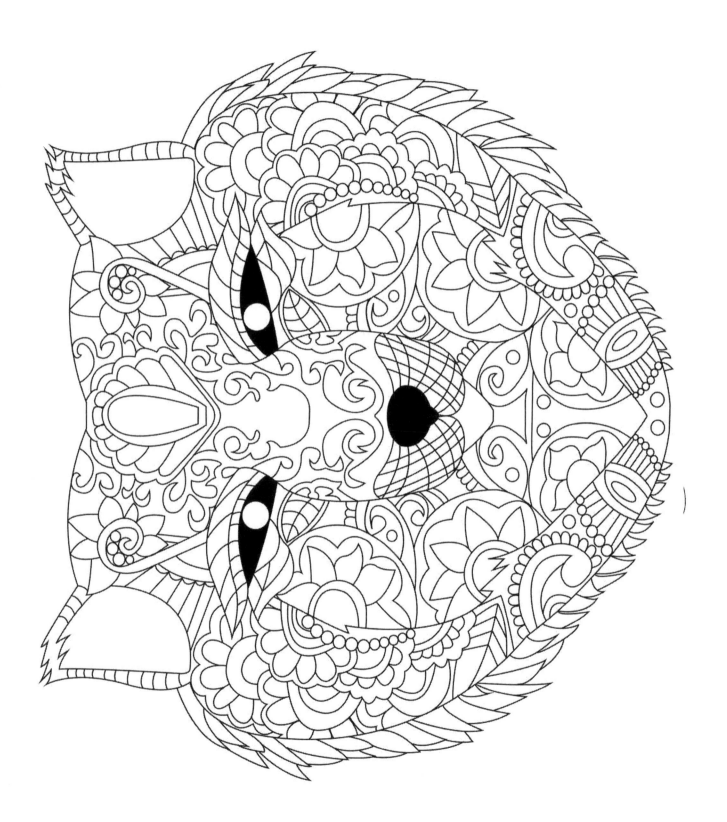

Printed in Poland
by Amazon Fulfillment
Poland Sp. z o.o., Wrocław